Those Eternally Linked Lives

Judy Hogan

For Susan, who knows
a lot about me, this
book might be
interesting."

Love,

Dad

1·23-18

ISBN: 978-1-945917-30-1

Printed in the United States of America

Cover Photo: *Bridges Two* © Julia Kennedy

Interior Images:
Orchid Buds © Rita Baldwin
Hand-Carved Finnish Bird at Book Party © Johnsie Tipton
Drawing of Bird Diving © Mikhail Bazankov
White Rock Hens © John Ewing

Big Table Publishing Company
Boston, MA
www.bigtablepublishing.com

Also by Judy Hogan

Poetry

Cassandra Speaking
Sun-Blazoned
Susannah, Teach Me to Love/Grace, Sing to Me
Light Food
Beaver Soul (Russian and English editions)
This River: An Epic Love Poem

Mysteries

The Sands of Gower: The First Penny Weaver Mystery
Haw: The Second Penny Weaver Mystery
Nuclear Apples? The Third Penny Weaver Mystery
Formaldehyde, Rooster: The Fourth Penny Weaver Mystery
Political Peaches: The Fifth Penny Weaver Mystery
Killer Frost: The Sixth Penny Weaver Mystery
Farm Fresh and Fatal: The Seventh Penny Weaver Mystery
Tormentil Hall: The Eighth Penny Weaver Mystery

Non-Fiction

Grace: A China Diary, 1910-16
Watering the Roots in a Democracy: A Manual On How to
Combine Literature and Writing in the Public Library
The Poor Woman's PMZ Cookbook: Vegetarian Recipes for Survival
and Health in the Menopausal and Post-Menopausal Years

For the village of Moncure, N.C., where, even in 2017, there exists real community. People help each other and still work together to stop harm coming to them as they have for decades. I'm proud to live here.

Table of Contents

Acknowledgements

Thanks to Doug Williams and Jerry Markatos for technical help with the photos, to Rita Baldwin for help with photographing orchid buds, to Julia Kennedy for letting us use on the cover her *Bridges 2* painting, the calendar art for May 2017, and for all my friends and neighbors who believe in me, trust me, and cheer me on. Robin of Big Table Publishing Company hung with me as we refined this book. I'm grateful to you all.

The Real Thing

There's no stopping spring once she stirs
to life all those roots under the soil cover.
Daffodils can weather ice. Peepers can go
back into their mud, but peach blossoms
come only once and kill so easily. Human
love has many changes it can ring. It can
spring to life and then die when reality
pricks its bubble. We sometimes see
and feel what we want to, and the other
person never stops being strange. Our
souls never fuse. When the real thing
happens, we may fight to get away.
We don't like feeling helpless or
taken captive by what we've seen and
loved. We don't realize how lucky we
are, when, all unaware, we start a fire
in another person's hearth. There's a
deeper wisdom at work, one that
throws off the conventional trappings
and goes for the knowing depths of
our souls, when one moment becomes
sufficient to last us a lifetime, no
matter the consequences. We prepare
to pay the costs even before we know
what they are. Only later do we realize
how lucky we are and how that love
sustained us and changed our lives.

I'm Speaking

You agreed: our story/our history
should be told. I wanted to give you
my heart whole, and I did. I couldn't
forget the high places where we rested
and were one, each having a wing. You
left the whole story to me. I held back
until now. If we soared, we also lost
ourselves in the tangled skein of anger,
scorn, tears, deadly silence. You could
silence me, whose one great need was
to speak. Since I'm alone now, I'm free
to tell it all: the agony and loss of
paradise, and its rediscovery. We were
fools, yet wiser than everyone around
us, living our lives as if we were one
bird, one flight, with only one home,
and that always together. The love
has outlasted your death. I'm aging
but I'm speaking. Once you would
have frowned at what I'm telling,
but now, from your new place of
contemplation, you're smiling.

No Regrets

When you left me, my heart was still whole
though you'd kept it safe while you were
alive. We both now depend on my heart
still beating, my writing hand and eye,
as good as ever. I return to my writings
of twenty-five years ago, relive my hunger
and your delight in me, and sometimes your
anger when you couldn't control my tears
or make me lift my head. Loving you was
never easy, but I regret nothing. I will
learn patience, not push myself so hard
that my heart rebels. In time I will publish
our story. For now, I slow myself down.
I always did win by persistence,
steady work, and my refusal to give up.
I know how to keep hope alive. Soon
I've lived and flourished eighty years.
I ask for twenty more to keep my heart
beating steadily as I work and rest, love
and let go, tell whole truths and keep
in my mind's eye our two wings
lifting us high at last.

Bridges

~ Looking at Julia Kennedy's painting, *Bridge #2*

Aging takes more work to keep my spirit strong.
Doubts sneak into my blind spot. I debate when
once I never would, so I need bridges. In May
I'll turn eighty years--four generations, one
more to go, I hope. This bridge takes me away
from rage and fear, those useless, even harmful
currents which distract me, rob my sleep, or seize
my brain for sleep when I fight to stay awake. Yet
blue rushes in to water these unwanted flames
before they do serious damage. It's the blue of
the ocean, of a river under full sun, or sky in the
fall of the year at sunset. Red is all too human
but weighs down the spirit. It's worth the
trouble to help these persistent streaks of
bright blue douse the flame that keeps us
uncertain where to place our feet.

Painting of Bridges by Julia Kennedy

Seeds

Spring, once it's official, rushes in,
heedless, yearning again toward green,
blooms, seeds. I can never keep up.
I turn eighty in two months when
these seeds will offer me peas, beets,
onions, lettuce. I didn't used to count
days, but now I do. Each day is a gift
we can't give back, can't save, can
only live as if it were our last. It
might be. Keep the heart beating
by using it and all my other muscles,
tendons, organs, nerves, bones. The
body is wedded to the soul. Keep
the soul happy, and the body will
flourish, hold off death, warm us
after a walk, sleep hard; and once
awake, find us plenty of puzzles to
solve and conflicts to agonize over.
Each time we penetrate fear, come
through those annoying, pesky doubts,
we re-find our balance, see light ahead,
not so terribly far off.

Beets and Onions in Spring

A Grace Mysterious

It's the buds I notice. The big orchid
in the window suddenly has them on
its rambling twigs as if it were hanging
paper lanterns out. The wild blackberry
that penetrated the orchard fence has
little white balls. The tips of the big
fig limbs are green, and the purple
shamrock hangs out its pink flower
bells. Can a nearly-eighty woman
bud, too? Can the solo cardinal's
trill give her soul in a new decade
a "go" signal. The red songster
doesn't worry how long he'll live,
but he's not planning books and
making lists. He doesn't have a
heart that insists "A day at a time,"
and makes no promises. I could
die tomorrow, though it's highly
unlikely. Love each day that brings
you back to life, see the bright green
chameleon running down the gray
chain-link fence. Remember all
the loves you have known in your
first eight decades. Hold no grudges.
From childhood you were sheltered
and nourished by a grace mysterious
and never named, but it opened
doors most people never see or
if they do, fear to open.

Orchid Buds by Rita Baldwin

Changing a Wrong to a Right

~ For Judge Carl Fox

You were told to hang on, and you did.
It took patience and a great faith to
sustain hope that a huge, rich public
utility company could be defeated by
a handful of determined citizens. You
worried for their health. Too many were
already sick and getting sicker from
coal ash toxins in the air. Wells were
poisoned. Risks were taken with
drinking water. All around us the
skeptics were immovable. "It's a done
deal." We were considered controversial
for demanding justice. Then a wise and
thoughtful judge told the truth. Dumping
coal ash was wrong; you have to stop.
No more trucks and trains, cutting trees
and digging holes. *Your permits are
revoked.* I was stunned, yet I saw for
the first time since this plan emerged:
truth and justice alive at last in a
court of law. The constitution remembered.
"Liberty and justice for all." We hugged
and told stories Ten of us who'd been
faithful, but many more helped, prayed,
gave us space to meet, to sing, sent
money for our lawyer. This small group
of concerned and committed citizens
did change a wrong to a right. We're

alert now. Best if the huge, rich, public
utility company sets aside its tricks
and begins to consider justice for its
customers and truth from its employees.
It's not too late.

Grandmother Grace Age 21

~ On the publication of *Grace: A China Diary, 1910-16*

Last night the first orchid bloomed, and
outside green was winning again: trees,
grass, fruit trees, seedlings, and healthy
weeds. Everything reborn, and I rise from
dreams that took me somewhere else until
I forgot this world, today, and how Easter
brings blooms. I have a good life, my own.
I took risks over and over. Wherever I
went, I found people to love, and now
I'm rich in friends. My writings are coming
into print, and my friends are buying
my books. I wanted to understand
Grandmother Grace's life, and now I do.
My friends want to understand, too. Grace's
sorrow took her mind away and others
inherited fear, fear of losing their minds.
I had fear, too, but I stayed my course,
kept up my courage, trusted my deep Self.
My wish and my kindness opened doors
others found locked and barred. I've
brought Grace and Harvey back to life,
not without pain and fear, but we're
assuaged now. My health holds. When
dreams take me away from myself, I
always return. I'm okay, now and
forever, and so is Grace.

Grandmother Grace Age 21

Two Graces

Could Grace be eternally linked, too?
I think so. Not on purpose. I didn't know
her when I was six and she was fifty-five.
She was home, not hospitalized then,
but whimsical and hard for Mother,
who was probably hard for her, and I
must have reminded her of her lost
child, Gracie, who died when she was
eight. There are the loves given to us
all unknowing, not planned, but something
deeper and kinder is at work, though
at age six it didn't feel kind. It felt scary.
Grace defied Mother and took Margie
and me to get our hair cut and permed.
Later she brought bunnies for Easter.
They lived outside and regularly
escaped into the local Victory gardens.
Mother had to chase them and bring
them back. For some reason I can't
fathom, my deep mind took in the two
Graces--maybe because they were models
that fitted--even though one was crazy
and the other one, dead. I had that same
sensitivity that makes an artist, which
Proust called *les grands nerveux*, or
neurotic. Too finely tuned not to care,
not to speak. I was sick but didn't die.
I was impulsive and bold, but didn't
go crazy, and only mildly neurotic.

Now I know why I must keep Grace
in my life. She was the artist who failed,
who had too much guilt and fear to fight
the rigidities in the world around her.
But I can lay my fears to rest. I've been
bold and openly loved whom I loved,
and now am speaking every truth I
see, and I know I'm sane. Furthermore
people listen. The orchid in my window
gives me a new bloom every day, and
my mind's depths offer revelations.

A Single Communion

Once you were alive and acting silly.
2001, when this photo was made
in the garden of Sveta's father, who
was dressed as a scarecrow. Marja-Sisko,
dear Finnish friend, on the other side of
our host, smiling. Behind us a lively
garden, some rows under row cover.
I was happy and stood close to you.
Sixteen years ago. We'd loved each
other eleven years, and sometimes
tried not to. It never worked. We each
played our parts. We had produced
our *Earth and Soul* anthology of North
Carolina poetry in English and Russian.
Copies went all over the Kostroma
Region to schools and libraries. Our
love was like that: almost all for
other people. For us a few moments
here and there of standing on that
precipice of ecstatic joy, clothed
in a single communion, words being
unnecessary. It began when we had
no words, two writers with no shared
speech. I learned Russian. Yet you
told me your love so many other
ways: gestures, laughter, funny faces,
silly songs, anger, drawings in that
very book we engineered together.

A man and woman stand before a
mountain they wish to climb and
leave their world behind, eat greens
and berries. It didn't matter. Arm in
arm, free. The walk we never took
but never forgot we wanted to.

Spring Re-surges

Slapped down by a Cold Front, Spring
re-surges; yellow green of new leaves;
purple-veined beet greens, lettuce leaves
crowded close. I pick my salad. The figs
undeterred. A few dead branches from
recent years' hard freezes don't discourage
them. Forsythia is resurrected; the
hydrangea's third crop of leaves is
still alive. I've made room for the
new iris bulbs. Bird song is early
because they're nesting, feeding young.
No time for love tunes. A freshening
wind as the sun pulls the earth back
to warmer soil, more blooms, and
swelling pea pods. All is steady,
safe, worries laid to rest. The dog
and I slept well. The sleep budget is
balanced. Evil men are doing harm,
but we will stop them, one at a time.
When you have justice on your side,
sooner or later you win, and if need
be, you win again and again.

Garden Peas

Such Perfect Love

How could I forget those days we spent
in my village when you came for two
weeks to North Carolina? We didn't
sleep together yet our spirits fused.
Your warm hands caressed my neck
when I was driving. You'd take me
to a large oak, take off your shoe, and
put your foot over mine while we prayed
to the spirit in the tree and over all.
Sometimes you were angry, or I was,
but you'd say we had to talk, and we
would. Such perfect love left us raw
when anger flared. We'd lose Paradise
and then re-find it. We tried to part,
but couldn't do it. So we carried each
other's souls the rest of our lives.
Your wife and son ministered to your
failing human body. You wrote one
letter after I sent you my love poem
This River. You were glad our story
was being told. Your wife forgives me.
So do her sons. Somehow, I added
richness to your life as you added grace
to mine. The mystery of such love is
never fully understood, but it stays.
I will never forget those hours and
days when our souls were simply one.
They still are.

Those Impossible Distances

My phalaenopsis orchid has twenty blooms,
each a revelation. All the green-white
lanterns have become exuberant faces,
winged like butterflies. Outside the window
green sweetgum stars flutter, then dance
when the wind picks up. Sometimes the
gods offer a miracle so easy to turn down.
It could never work. It isn't enough. We
did wish for more, yet to connect as we
did kept us safe and happy. If sometimes
sad, yet out of despair. We were too busy
flinging ourselves those impossible
distances to grieve at what wasn't possible,
given who we were and what we valued:
truth and faithfulness, joy in helping others
see what we saw. Since you died, there
are new shadows. A great darkness hovers:
cruel, making hatred seem normal, claiming
evil is good and good is evil. The human
spirit has been here before. We know how
to die if we have to. Meantime we keep
singing our hymn to liberty, justice, and
mutual love.

Sun Again

The peas are nearly finished. I pick
beet leaves, half-grown lettuce,
two firm bright green peppers, fronds
of lemon balm and peppermint for
tea. The hens gave me seven eggs.
Sun again after so much rain brings
out tiny bumps that will be figs by
August. I hack at poison ivy, pull
handfuls of bamboo grass, mow
the backyard where Wag's vole
holes outdo the grass. Dale comes
to change my flat tire, puts on
the spare. I drive thirty miles for
the flat to be repaired. Harold mows
more of my yard than I had managed
and leaves before I can thank him.
Birthday wishes come by mail,
e-mail, and phone. The waves I
make in the wider world are scarcely
noticed, but I fall asleep reassured
that I'm doing what I need to do.
My less reliable memory is good
enough. Everything I do counts
in the long tabulation of the
centuries. "Be of good cheer,"
sounds in my ears. Sun reigns.

One White Rock Hen

Intangible Communion

We each had a hand-crafted Finnish bird—
mid-flight. Snow goose or swan? You bought
two. One for me in my village; one for your
apartment in town, which I saw when we
drove home from your village. You had been
cruel and angry, only a little less as we
traveled. That day the bird told me everything
I needed to know. It still does now that I
live in another house, another village. Sometimes
what's tangible reinforces what we can't
touch or know with absolute certainty.
Belief is all we have and then that knowledge
that makes proof irrelevant—some direct
seeing that passes all the roadblocks and
doubts. Of course there are skeptics, and
sometimes we're assailed by doubts, too.
But the bird persists. One look reminds
us. You're not there in your town or village
any more, but this bird here has its
continuing message as it moves in the
fan's wind: "I'm still here. I'm inside you.
Heart to heart is what matters." For us
that part was easy. The hard part was
opening such a truth to other people
when they can't imagine
such intangible communion.

That Tide of Growth

It rains, and green surges. I can't
keep up. I engage with deeply rooted
weeds and mud. The work I need to do
is everywhere visible. The orchid is casting
its blooms. Ten months until they come
again. Human effort feels so small against
that tide of growth. Simple sun and rain
send green hurtling forward. Sweetgum
stars obscure my view out the window.
Yet the self-heal blooms; the daylilies
make each day new. Later too much heat
will slow things down. Wet soil helps
me yank out the worst weeds. The hens
are happy, making their straw into new
nests, the wet earth sending more bugs
to the surface. Sometimes it's hard
when so much is up to me. Yet I flourish,
walk, eat, and sleep well; thread my way
through difficulties; ask help; do my
part as the days allow. When I can't
see very far ahead, I hold on. I've
been in so many dark places before.
Light always finds me sooner or later
if I keep myself from despair.

Self-Heal Plants in Early Spring

Hang on for a Rough Ride

The tallest tree–the tulip–shimmers in
a world of green. Vines climb the fences.
My flower garden weeds are three feet
high, the perennials higher. Daylilies had
to fight off bamboo grass. The figs have
so many leaves I can't see the dead
branches, and I know those infant knobs
are swelling. A day finally dawned without
rain. Soon I can mow, and tackle the
high weeds. The hens took it all in stride.
Muddy, bedraggled feathers were clean
and white again when the new day arrived.
Even in human beings life renews itself.
Sleep heals; dreams restore our cells and
our souls. We are new again every day.
One look out the window, and we know
what we have to do. This life is not for
the faint of heart. We let go only what
we must; hang on for a rough ride, remount
our courage and listen to our hearts. It's
the only way to stay whole and keep our
true Selves intact until we die and see
that Death is still some distance off.

Flock of White Rock Hens

Steady on my Course

In all this growth of green—vines, grasses,
fig leaves and tiny figs, the tall swaying
tulip tree, the grass I need to cut, the iris
and daylilies holding their own against
bamboo grass—where is the grace that will
hold me steady on my own course, the one
I chose, not going against the universe's
grain, but having to tolerate fear in others
for me and hatred when I succeed; even awe
when I defy the doctors' wisdom. How
can I be still young, my flesh still firm; my
heart holding its own. Banishing fear has
become a habit. Every time I outwit other
people's worries, I stand taller in my own
view. All it takes is courage, helping those
who let me, and taking in gratefully those
loving hands that give me a reason
to stay alive.

Figs in August

Against the Odds

I knew, when I wished to live
a long time, that, as I approached
a hundred years, living would
become more difficult. Even as
my body ages well, it is more
vulnerable, needs more care,
its regular exercise, healthy diet,
and for its sleep budget to be
balanced. I have my commitments
I can't say no to, for myself and
my writings, for my children and
friends, and for my community
here in Moncure. It has always
been a balancing act–never more so
than now. I hold my own, but it
takes more ingenuity to outwit
my gradual aging and the deadly
poisons let loose in our twenty-first
century world, out to kill us and
destroy our hope. The answer is
simple and obvious: in our deep
souls we know we can't be seriously
harmed if we refuse despair. Insights
will arrive. Courage will appear
against the odds. The grain of the

universe doesn't go away. Furthermore
other people gather around us, one
at a time. If we ask, we receive, and
not infrequently, we receive the help
we need before we ask.

Still Here

Even if the brakes are being put on
slowly, we know the end of our lives
will come. We can't be blithe as
once; yet we can live as normally
and joyfully as possible. The doctors
are not worried. Their tests reassure
them that my heart jumping around
and out of its steady rhythm for an
hour can be lived with. For me it is
an unmistakable sign to pay attention:
walk, yes; work, write, dig. See to
the hens, mow and weed-eat; lead
my village in the fight to stop a
coal ash dump, but rest and eat
well, stay alert, respect the signs
as you accumulate years. You
can't have enough courage or of
the vision that shows you your way,
a step at a time. You're still here,
aren't you? Still thriving, loving
those who let you, filling each
day with work completed? Your
conscience is clear; you see all
too well into the hearts of others
whether they imagine yours or not.

Flowers and Brownies

Gifts

It will be nineteen years in December
that I have lived in this small house in
Moncure with a garden, an orchard, and
a small flock of hens. I'd already then
been given many gifts: by a banker, who
outwitted the mortgage rules; by friends
who helped paint and weed-eat and
move a big pile of bricks, which became
my flower garden. Even before I moved
in, I joined the fight to stop a low-level
nuclear dump. We did stop it. Then we
stopped three attempts to site a landfill
and ended ten years of bad air pollution.
I worked to elect more careful county
commissioners, then to keep out fracking,
and since 2014, coal ash. This time
they pushed in before we could stop
them. It took a judge to halt that, but
they're holding off our justice again.
I hold steady, but more problems have
surfaced: my water heater quit; my
heart began racing; now it's high
heat warnings keeping me inside
while the weeds flourish. Yet people
turn up to help me: Mike, to challenge
the water heater's diagnosis; Harold
to mow; Merle, bringing tomatoes
when my bushes stopped producing

shortly after they began. Then two
men from my electric coop got
the water heater back on track. Many
helpers when I needed them. Everyone
has annoying problems, but I'm older;
so is my water heater and my farm.
Despite unruly weeds and heat,
the figs, grapes, and apples are plentiful.
Some rain would help, and cooler weather.
All this help puzzles me, though I'm very
grateful. Then it hits me. I wanted to
create an island of sanity and love. Looks
like I did, despite the weeds, my aging
body and what belongs to me. The big
world does grow more difficult, but in my
world there definitely is sanity and love.

Enough!

The tree we made between
us seeded itself and new flowers
open like white dogwood in North
Carolina, tight knobs while Spring
hesitates; then open-handed once
She makes up Her mind, their
petals reminding us of where, once,
the hands of a good man were
nailed to a tree. Goodness is always
going to suffer in our world, but if
goodness seeded itself, and new
trees grow, and new flowers open,
and new springs give new cause
to laugh and delight in one another,
to speak the heart's truth knowing
the other listens and cares, it is
enough. . .
       You said that one must travel
a long road to reach the heart.
How far have we come now?
I can't remember very well the
beginning. We opened our souls' doors
to each other freely then. We laughed
and we were sad. You said, when
I left, "It's only a light sadness,
Judy." Soon I leave again. For me
the sadness I feel has never been
light, though I carried it easily.

What choice did I have? No one
knows how much we say to one
another when we don't speak a word.
　　　From Sun 20, December 1995

Did we reach the heart? I think so.
We both had many claims on our lives,
but from the first hours we wanted to
give everything we had to give. Later we
learned our limits and the long road
appeared. We said nothing would
hinder us—neither the thousands of miles,
our lifestyle differences, nor the language
barrier. Yet all those had their power to
impede the flow of a love we could
neither deny nor let govern our lives.
It's one way for souls to fuse: when
there's no other alternative. Our love
became a powerful force in fostering
understanding between two distinct
and very different cultures. Despite
our suffering we did not only reach
each other's hearts, we stayed there.
The little wooden bird you gave me
still flies. When the light is right, its
shadow dances on the filing cabinet.

I still see you in my mind's eye, feel
your tight hug as you whisper: "You're
a hero." Hear your laughter: "We were
fools!" Then you added: "And miracle
workers." I can ask no better gift
than to have traveled that long road
to rest safely in your heart.

Things Change

We forget: things change all the time.
People change their minds. Our
weather changes. Chickens like their
routines, but they change where they
roost, sometimes hide their nests.
On an old farm, despite neglect,
things grow. A Rose of Sharon leans
through the fence to say hello. Little
blue flowers appear on the Wandering
Jew. Figs ripen and some spoil from
all the rain. After a slew of problems,
a respite: a gift I'd given up on,
forgotten. I got hurt, but I've been
healing. I spoke some hard truth,
and was invited to speak again. I'll
have students in September. My soul
settled in for my older age. I have
to consider my heart, my balance, and
how easily I forget. The weeds feel
impossible, but I know how to summon
helping hands. Wag and I do our daily
walk steadily. I work on manuscripts
I'm determined to publish; plant a few
more beans, find enough figs to sell.
My life resumes its normal rhythms.
Rain replaces the heat wave.
My soul is peaceful once again.

People Care

I do keep staying alive. I could have died
on Monday. Instead I fell as I raced
across the road to avoid a speeding car.
She wasn't looking, she said. She stopped,
pulled me off the road, called nine-one-one.
Other cars stopped, including a sheriff's
deputy. Then the fire department and
two ambulances. I recognized the voices
of David and Jerry. Claudia came up.
I asked her to put Wag behind the fence.
Later she came back to pray with me.
The phone kept ringing even during the
prayer. I did hit my head. A scalp wound
bled. John Bonitz called. Was I okay?
He heard a car hit me. No, I fell, but
she could have. I'm okay. Sheila called
to say she and Rhonda were coming
over. Then John and Wayne Cross
stopped to check on me. Emails and
phone calls. Rhonda checked my scalp:
"It will heal." Jeff took me to pick up
my truck. Emma stopped by, having
heard the rumor. Sally wrote from Alabama.
Katie, from Asheville. Then Keely, Donna,
and Terica brought me groceries. Maybe
I couldn't get to a store? Fruit and other
things I never buy on my simple diet,
but I'm enjoying them. Angelina says,

"You could use this in a novel. I keep
telling people the car didn't hit you."
What did hit me was people's care:
 I had to be all right. I am. Healing
well; reminding my children I want
to stay independent, follow my deep
wisdom. Falling's no fun, but once
again, I learned: people love me.

Some Things the Memory Won't Let Go Of

Finally, a letter from Yuri–three
typed pages, but my Russian is
half-forgotten. I get out my big
dictionary. When I wrote to him
in late June, I'd been reading my
diary pages from when I'd stayed
with him and Vera twenty-two years
ago. He congratulates me on my
Jubilee–eighty years–most of them
writing. How they nurtured me back
then, and they're still alive. We both
lost Mikhail, whom he calls Misha,
and sends me a note he wrote Misha
a month before he died. They both
longed for their childhood villages–
gone now but never forgotten. Yuri
remembers the yellow flowers under
the cottage's window. Mikhail remembers
 being put upon a horse and seeing a
pink sky, then falling off the horse.
A recurring theme everywhere I went:
the lost village, the *rodina*, birth village,
lost and never forgotten. A holy grail
to those who remember. He kept taking
me to see the village houses. Once I
stayed in one. He took me into the *taiga*,
the wild forest, where his village had

been until lost because of the push for
communal farms, and then the war
when twenty-seven million died
in battle or in prison camps. Some
things the memory won't let go of,
as long as we breathe. We still love
those who loved us, and to whom
we opened our souls. It's called:
reaching the heart.

Courage

I heal. Again. Courage found and
rewarded. I rise to my problems.
One at a time I'll overcome
both my new and my old fears.
We have cooler days and nights.
I can work outside more often.
Sun is less of a threat. My son
calls to say he may be able to
move here sooner rather than
later. I rejoice. I am confident
we can work out and through
the minor problems, if he finds
his way to returning home. I
Already have good help, but the
thought of his near presence
comforts me in a new way. He
has respect for my independence,
but he wants to help. I stayed
unbiased while he wrestled with
it, but finally said, "If you can
work it out, I'll be glad." The
mysterious partner inside me
is grateful. This counts, too, and
helps me finish my work on earth.

Drawing of Bird Diving by Mikhail Bazankov

Weathering Storms

Sun is back after our storms
that flung down dead branches
but watered the grapes, zinnias, and okra.
I revel in three zinnias, their petals
fanned out to imitate suns, and I eat
five okra, some so tough only the seeds
are edible. I make tea from my huge
crop of lemon balm, and the dog and I
resume our normal walk. We both
sleep hard these days and have less
patience. I can tell I'm healing. I'm
not ready to be put on a shelf. It's
up to me to keep up the yard,
check on the hens, keep my active
healthy lifestyle. Aging takes courage
in a new way. Other people worry
and need reassurance. When she took
my heart's pictures, I could hear
its steady beat. I've had doctors
try to slow me down before, but
the wise ones listen to me. Trust
myself. I feel good, normal. Worry
wears down the soul. Let it go.
Move the dead branches. Watch
for the zinnias to rise again. Check
the grapes and okra. You know how
to weather the storms, in the sky,
and in your soul.

Zinnias on the Kitchen Table

Reason to be Happy

Slowly, I clear weeds, pick grapes,
cook out the juice and make Muscadine
jelly. The hens get the grapes. They
lay better. The zinnias rise again
and bloom. The spider lilies make their
annual surprise and throw up exultant
pink petals and whiskers. The next door
cats make friends with Wag. Are they
keeping warm together at night?
Arching over the garden weeds are
sunny yellow flowers. I forget their
name, and the rainbow lantana. The
high grasses aren't dwarfed but have
competition. Reckless pink
morning glories cover the porch
railing, determined to cheer me up.
My heart is pronounced normal.
I heal and resume more work as
the air cools. I tackle the high
grass a little at a time. My students
bring laughter and comfort. Observation
wins over theory. I have every reason
on earth to be happy and brave.

An Inner Guide

When you have an inner guide, be
thankful. You know how to go it
alone. You listen to those who
care and worry about you, but
ultimately, it's up to you as you
enter that stage of your life when
more losses will come your way.
For eighty you're not doing too
badly. As it gets harder, you find
the grit you need to hold your own.
"A day at a time" is always a good
approach. Keep listening to your
deep wisdom. It has never let you
down. Your own individual path
is well-marked now, but such paths
always throw up something new.
Not everyone is up for the wholly
new, but you are. Keep yourself
fit and happy. Enjoy the orange
zinnia that survived the dog's vole
digging and being bent down by
the wind only to rise and flourish
anyway. Take a leaf out of *that* book.

The Way the Universe Is Made

I'm the vessel, the way our story
will be told, is already being told.
Two books in print and more coming.
You can't help except maybe by
your voice planted deep in my
memory. "We were fools, Judy,
and miracle-workers." Now my
country makes out your country
as an enemy. Yuri was worried:
what if Americans used nuclear
weapons against Russia? I write
to save one human experience
that will make war-mongering
irrelevant. The human race has
brought on itself huge and
devastating storms; floods,
drought. Yet we two believed
God helped us. Not a personal
god, but the way the universe
is made. Evil exists, but it wins
only if we let it. The universe's
binding of our two souls taught
us where the real power lies. We
are helpless only if we say we
are. We get reminders of our
frailty and then of our strength.
The zinnias I planted barely
survived, but the lantana and

the small sunflowers took over,
and the forgotten naked ladies.
Pink morning glories ran over
the back porch railing. Cosmos
leaped into the air from the
unweeded garden. I set my
worries aside. Rejoiced when
editors I've never met want to
read about my love for a Russian
man that leapt over all the
boundaries of time and distance,
language, lifestyle. Metaphors
carried us past all the gate-keepers.
We had our wings–in-spirit, and
our souls fused. If the spirit is happy
in its dwelling place, the body will
keep up as best it can. After all, what
is eternity but that which flies beyond
all the human definitions of stopping
places. Let me die only when my
story–our story–is alive for the whole
human race to treasure and save.

About the Author

Judy Hogan was co-editor of a poetry journal (Hyperion, 1970-81). In 1976 she founded Carolina Wren Press. She has been active in central North Carolina as a reviewer, book distributor, publisher, teacher, and writing consultant.

Seven mystery novels, *Killer Frost* (2012), *Farm Fresh and Fatal* (2013) *The Sands of Gower* (2015), *Haw, Nuclear Apples? Formaldehyde, Rooster* (2016), *Political Peaches* (2017) are in print. *Tormentil Hall* comes out March 1, 2018. She has published six other volumes of poetry with small presses, including, *Beaver Soul* (2013) and *This River: An Epic Poem* (2014). Her published prose is: *Grace: A China Diary*, 1910-16 (2017) *Watering the Roots in a Democracy* (1989) and *The PMZ Poor Woman's Cookbook* (2000). Her papers and 25 years of extensive diaries are in the Sallie Bingham Center for Women's History and Culture, Duke University. She has taught creative writing since 1974 and Freshman English 2004-2007 at St. Augustine's College in Raleigh.

Between 1990 and 2007 she visited Kostroma, Russia, five times, teaching American literature at Kostroma University in 1995 and giving a paper to a Kostroma University Literature Conference in March 2007. She worked on five exchange visits, as well as cooperative publishing with Kostroma writers and exhibits of their artists. Judy lives and farms in Moncure, N.C., near Jordan Lake.